British Legends: The Life and Legacy of Sean Connery

By Charles River Editors

Sean Connery at the 1988 Academy Awards

About Charles River Editors

Charles River Editors was founded by Harvard and MIT alumni to provide superior editing and original writing services, with the expertise to create digital content for publishers across a vast range of subject matter. In addition to providing original digital content for third party publishers, Charles River Editors republishes civilization's greatest literary works, bringing them to a new generation via ebooks.

Introduction

Sean Connery (1930-)

"I suppose more than anything else I'd like to be an old man with a good face, like Hitchcock or Picasso. They know that life is not just a popularity contest." – Sean Connery, 1964

A lot of ink has been spilled covering the lives of history's most influential figures, but how much of the forest is lost for the trees? In Charles River Editors' British Legends series, readers can get caught up to speed on the lives of Britain's most important men and women in the time it takes to finish a commute, while learning interesting facts long forgotten or never known.

Perhaps no actor has been able to retain their popularity into old age as well as Sean Connery. Despite retiring in 2006, Connery remains a venerable figure who continued to receive accolades for his handsome virility and status within the Hollywood elite. After all, in 1989, just shy of his 60th birthday, Connery was feted by People magazine as the Sexiest Man Alive, and in the years that followed, Connery was awarded with even more lifetime achievement awards, including being named Sexiest Man of the Century by People magazine in 1999. As an actor, Connery won an Academy Award for his performance in The Untouchables (1989), and he has also been awarded Golden Globes and BAFTA awards as well. Based on these designations, one can reasonably place Connery among the ranks of the most acclaimed Hollywood actors of all time, a figure whose critical reputation only grew as he matured.

Considering his personal acclaim as an actor, it is perhaps surprising that despite his status, most of the films in which Connery has appeared are not particularly acclaimed. Indeed, scanning his filmography, viewers finds very few films that have been showered with any significant awards, and even the role that brought Connery to fame, the James Bond franchise, initially received a largely lukewarm critical reception. On occasion, Connery has worked with directors of great critical standing, most notably Alfred Hitchcock in *Marnie* (1963), and yet even these films were not greeted with great praise. While Connery's skills as an actor remain unquestioned, his films themselves have not been canonized as outstanding, nor do they populate the curricula of film courses.

  Given the gulf between Connery's own reputation and those of his films, it is natural to conclude that Connery's fame has arisen despite appearing in films that were generally unworthy of his talents as an actor. One of the prevailing questions surrounding Connery, therefore, is how he was able to attain such fame and acclaim despite appearing in films that have continually been deemed less than outstanding. To answer that question, it is necessary to consider not only his film appearances but also the personal background that shaped his career decisions and contributed to the development of his star persona. In fact, the legend of Sean Connery is inseparable from his upbringing, as well as the precarious period of his young adulthood. Connery came from an impoverished background, and his willingness later in his career to accept roles that were seemingly beneath him can be attributed to a blue collar ethos that respects the value and importance of hard work. In light of his difficult upbringing, Connery's rise to stardom is an unlikely one, as Connery managed to progress from the poorest regions of Edinburgh, Scotland to the heights of Hollywood fame, becoming famous for his signature mix of suave, debonair comportment and virile masculinity. At the same time, Connery's eccentric behavior in later years, which might be criticized if other people acted that way, are often considered part of the unique Connery charm.

  British Legends: The Life and Legend of Sean Connery looks at the life of the iconic Bond actor on and off the silver screen. Along with pictures of important people, places, and events, you will learn about Sean Connery like you never have before, in no time at all.

Chapter 1: Hard Work and Little Pay

"I am not an Englishman, I was never an Englishman, and I don't ever want to be one. I am a Scotsman! I was a Scotsman and I will always be one." – Sean Connery

Thomas Sean Connery's upbringing could not have been more unassuming. Although it is uncertain when exactly he started using his middle name as a first name, he was called Tommy as a child and went by Thomas or "Big Tam" throughout adolescence. Connery later claimed friends started calling him Sean because he also had an Irish friend named Séamus, but in any event, he had been named Thomas after his grandfather.

Connery was born in Fountainbridge, an impoverished and rough area of Edinburgh, Scotland, and the fact that Connery was raised in Scotland and not England became all the more significant when he would later become a fierce advocate and financial contributor for the Scottish National Party. He was born on August 25, 1930, the first child of parents James and Elizabeth (Effie), who had been married since December 28, 1928. Thomas was a large baby, weighing between 10 and 11 pounds, and his substantial size was inherited from his parents. His father Joe was a short, stocky man, while his mother Effie had a towering presence that made her appear far taller than her husband (Yule).

What the Connery family lacked in wealth they made up for in brawn, and Sean was born into a characteristically hearty and fiery Scottish family. At the time of his birth, Joe worked as a laborer at the North British Rubber Company Mill, a menial position for which he was paid two pounds per week (Bray). Effie did not work and instead raised her child, though she would later work as a maid. Their class status was also reflected by the fact that the dynamic between her and Joe was patriarchal. He was a full six years older than her, and the differences between the two referred to more than just age. Neither came from an affluent background, but Effie's family was of considerably higher standing than that of Joseph, whose parents were Roman Catholic and had not been married. In fact, none of the Connerys (including Joe) had ever learned to read, whereas Effie's family was Protestant and she had received a basic education. Perhaps unsurprisingly given their different backgrounds, the two extended families did not get along amicably, and Joseph would later state only half-jokingly that a riot nearly ensued at their wedding (Bray).

Even if the extended families never got along, every indication suggests that Sean's parents generally got along well and were content to live in conditions that were sometimes severely destitute (Bray). The family lived in Fountainbridge, one of the most heavily impoverished regions of Edinburgh, in an Irish and Scottish neighborhood nicknamed "Old Smoke" during the 18th century. The neighborhood's name came from the many factories in the area, which employed the residents but also made for rather unpleasant living conditions. However, even as they were faced with conditions that would be considered unacceptable for many, the family enjoyed the neighborhood. The residents of Fountainbridge were united by their collective adversity, forming a surrogate extended family that effectively took the place of the fractured one that actually existed among the two sides of Sean's family.

Even so, anecdotes relayed by Sean years later reveal a living situation that was less than pleasant. As a young child, his family could not afford a crib, so he was instead relegated to sleeping in one of the drawers of his parents' wardrobe (Callan), and the living quarters were so cramped that all the families on the floor of his apartment had to share the same bathroom (Parker). Making matters worse, Joe had great difficulty maintaining employment, bouncing from one menial job to the next (Bray). Despite their lack of funds, however, Effie was adept at handling money, and the Connery household managed to survive.

As a young child, Sean was relatively happy, but he was oversensitive and clashed with his father from a young age. Joe grew frustrated by his inability to continuously provide for his family and was temperamental as a result, which led to Sean developing a closer relationship with his mother. It is not difficult to see why Sean was closer to Effie than Joe for other reasons too, since she preached the values of education and was more nurturing, in stark contrast with Joe's blue collar and fiery temper. Furthermore, during Sean's infancy Joe was scarcely at home, because he took on as much overtime as physically possible. It is no exaggeration to state that he spent more time at work than at home, and his contribution to Sean's upbringing was far more financial than affectionate.

Young Sean Connery

Sean attended the Bruntsfield Primary School, where he was a decent student who displayed a strong intelligence and had little difficulty becoming the first Connery to learn to read. At the same time, however, he had great difficulty adhering to the disciplined nature of the classroom; he had inherited Joe's restless physical energy and found the classroom constraining (Callan). Although he was generally small as a young child, he had a growth spurt in his early teens that would see him propel to the 6'2 stature known around the world today, and he put his physicality to good use while playing sports such as soccer. However, he was also eager to test the limits of acceptable behavior, and on one occasion he was even brazen enough to shoplift while in the presence of his mother (Bray). It seemed that Sean displayed an occasionally unsteady balance of sensitivity and aggression, inheriting the dominant aspects of both Joe and Effie's personalities.

Connery as a teenager

In the Connery household, socioeconomic progress was measured through the size of one's family, so it was the longtime goal of Joe and Effie to give birth to another child. In 1938, when Sean was 8 years old, his brother Neil was born. However, the decision to have a second child would hamstring the family financially, especially after Joe hurt himself and was physically incapacitated for 18 months. In order to support the family, Sean and Effie both had to work, with the young boy finding employment with St. Cuthbert's Dairy Stables as a milk delivery boy. The job would have a profound impact on Sean, who would work on and off at St. Cuthbert's for the next 8 years. Although the work was strenuous, the job was a good fit for him, and the job strengthened his love for horses and nurtured his love for farm life. Additionally, the physical nature of the work offered an appealing antidote to the stifling environment of the classroom. Sean would awaken at dawn and deliver milk before heading to school; after his studies were completed for the day, he would then work as a butcher's helper (Callan). These jobs did not pay handsomely, but the 3 pounds per week he earned went directly to the family, and his contribution was integral in providing for the family while his father was incapacitated.

Sean was also well-suited for the physical nature of his job at the Dairy Stables since he grew at an alarmingly fast rate. He inherited his mother's height and towered over his comparably diminutive father by the time he was 18. The rapid growth in height made him excessively gangly, but working on the farm also rounded out his physique. The lifestyle was tiring, but it exemplified the extent to which he applied the principles of hard work inherited from his father.

As a boy, Connery may have been more of a student than his parents, but it was also clear that he was more laborer than scholar. As a result, he made the decision to attend the Darroch Secondary School, a vocational institution, rather than enrolling in the more academically-focused Boroughmuir School. This decision was not only informed by his own preference for labor over the classroom but also due to the cultural climate of his Edinburgh neighborhood. It was expected that the local school kids would grow up following in their parents' footsteps and become laborers, and the notion of remaining in a classroom through the age of 18 was difficult to rationalize in the eyes of many, particularly when the teen had already grown to an adult size by the age of 13. If anything, it was only natural that Sean terminate his formal education at a relatively young age, and he turned his attention to manual labor.

Analyzing Connery's upbringing, it is easy to come to the conclusion that he was forced into working at too young an age. Certainly, his days were intimidating for the sheer amount of physical exertion involved, and he worked every bit as hard as his father had done during his own early years. However, Connery was not opposed to work, and he had a close, nurturing relationship with his mother. When he was 16, she used her savings to buy him a motorcycle, and shortly thereafter, he used his own savings to buy a piano. Even though he continued to contribute the majority of his earnings to his parents, he was endowed with the freedom and ability to make substantial purchases of his own choosing. Connery's upbringing may have been strenuous, but it was not abusive, and it supplied him with the strict work ethic he would maintain as an adult.

Chapter 2: Armed Forces

"I haven't found anywhere in the world where I want to be all the time. The best of my life is the moving. I look forward to going." – Sean Connery

Connery would later assert, "Your background and environment is with you for life. No question about that." But even though Connery always felt a sense of both nationalism and kinship with his neighborhood, his restless sensibility made him want to leave the neighborhood as he became a young adult. Living quarters at home were tight; not only was the apartment small, but Joe's injuries often forced him to stay home and Sean's younger brother Neil was still a relatively small child. Making matters worse, the fact that Joe was unable to provide for the family gave him something of an inferiority complex, especially in comparison with Sean's able-bodied frame.

Unfortunately for Sean, however, he had very few actual opportunities for leaving the house. In the absence of a full high school education, it was impossible for him to enter college. Meanwhile, the poor economy in Fountainbridge left him with no legitimate careers that would provide him with the financial means necessary to leave his household. As a result, Connery decided to enter the armed forces, enlisting in 1947 at the age of just 17. He signed a 12-year commitment that entailed seven as a sailor and five in the Naval Reserve (Bray), later explaining, "I left Scotland when I was 16 because I had no qualifications for anything but the Navy, having left school at 13."

At the time in which Connery enlisted in the armed forces, he was in many ways psychologically unprepared for the rigors of the lifestyle. His life had been physically demanding and filled with adversity from an early age, but he had also had no troubles socially yet. As a result, the unjust social dynamics of the Navy made him especially uneasy, because the Royal Navy adhered to a rigid class structure that privileged those who came from socioeconomically affluent backgrounds. Connery's impoverished upbringing left him at the bottom rung of the social ladder, and he was essentially treated as persona non grata (Bray). Connery would later complain, "I just think the most difficult thing to displace is privilege."

Furthermore, Connery had never been away from home, and even though he was ready to move out of the house, he was unready for the harsh environment to which he was subjected. He quickly grew homesick, and shortly after entering the Navy, he obtained two tattoos, one that said "Scotland Forever" and another stating "Mum and Dad." That Connery got tattoos after entering the Navy would not appear significant - tattoos are quite common among sailors - but his reasons for doing so were vastly different from those of most sailors. Connery's tattoos were expressions of his homesickness, reflecting a deep-rooted desire to return to the past. When his conditions vis-a-vis the other sailors failed to improve, he realized that remaining in the armed services would be untenable, particularly for the lengthy 12-year term to which he was contractually obligated.

The exact circumstances of Connery's experience in the Navy remain unclear, and Connery has quite understandably been reticent to disclose the full details associated with his Navy experience, but however it happened, he was honorably discharged just 17 months after entering the Navy. He was discharged due to a duodenal ulcer, and the legitimacy of this discharge is a topic for debate, since some people believe it's possible Connery feigned illness as a recourse through which to leave the service. With that said, ulcers were prevalent throughout his father's side of the family, so Connery may have suffered from ulcers himself or he may have used his father's medical history as a convenient means through which to exit an environment he found particularly hostile.

With no options for employment readily available upon leaving the Navy, the 19 year old was forced to return to his parents' apartment in Fountainbridge. He may have failed in his intended career as a sailor, but he was still entering the prime of his life and young enough to explore diverse employment opportunities. At the same time, he was constrained by the poor economy of Fountainbridge and had difficulty securing any form of lasting employment. In this regard, he was crucially helped by receiving a military pension, even though the sum was hardly enough to sustain himself on and he would need to find gainful employment.

Due to the lack of decent job opportunities, the list of occupations Connery held for the first three years following his discharge is immense. Immediately following his return to Fountainbridge, he worked at St. Cuthbert's Dairy, but considering that he had first worked at that dairy farm all the way back when he was 9 years old, it was easy for Connery to feel as though his life had failed to progress. In this regard, Christopher Bray notes, "The fact was that the headstrong purchase of the piano aside, joining the Navy had been the only real decision Tam Connery had made for himself. And it had not worked out. A couple of years after signing on, he was back on his parents' couch with nothing to show for his adventure but a 6s 8d (33p) a week pension. And what 18-year-old wants to be known as an invalid?"

Connery also worked a number of menial jobs in addition to his stint at St. Cuthbert's Dairy, but he had difficulty finding anything fulfilling. It would be unfair to attribute his lack of success to lack of ambition, since he had inherited his father's work ethic, but at this point in time it seemed Sean would be stuck toiling in a factory and following in his father's footsteps.

Oddly enough, his path out of that lifestyle would come because of his burgeoning interest in a new hobby: bodybuilding. Even though Connery had a tall frame, he was still somewhat slight, and his experience in the Navy had made him self-conscious about his lack of muscle. Bodybuilding also provided him with a productive means through which to process and literally work out the anxieties of underemployment. As it would turn out, the transformation of Connery's physique helped him find more fulfilling employment working as a male model for the Edinburgh College of Art. Even though the job was only temporary and paid just 15 shillings per hour, it made him increasingly cognizant of his physical attributes (Yule). In the Navy, he had been undersized compared to his peers, but after strength training, he acquired the virile physique that would later serve him to great effect in the film industry. Despite having no training in modeling, Connery was well-regarded by the art students, one of whom, Rich Demarco, later said that Connery was "very straight, slightly shy, too, too beautiful for words, a virtual Adonis."

Another fortuitous development that occurred around this time was that the British Legion offered to subsidize continuing education for war veterans, so long as the courses were vocational in nature. In a surprising decision, Connery opted to learn the art of French polishing at Vinestock in the East of Edinburgh. While seemingly insignificant, this career choice would prove influential in the chain of events that would culminate in Connery becoming an actor. One of Connery's classmates, Peter Moran, came from a well-off family and befriended Connery. The pairing was a fortunate one for Connery, who by this time was already in his early 20s and had yet to spend any time in a big city outside of his brief stint with the Navy. But with Moran, he ventured into London and became enchanted with the feel of his new surroundings. Although he was unable to move to London at that point in time, his first exposure to London ensured that Connery would make it a goal to return.

Ultimately, the furniture polishing job was short-lived, and even though Connery set his sights on returning to London, no immediate opportunities were available there, so he accepted a seasonal position as a lifeguard in Edinburgh. Connery's time weightlifting and playing soccer served him well in this role, and the amount of attention he got from young ladies ensured that he remained self-conscious about his body. This only compelled him to exercise that much more, and when he was not on duty at the pool, he spent considerable time working out. If anything, playing soccer ensured that Connery didn't get too muscular, but he was so good at both soccer and bodybuilding that he started to enter bodybuilding competitions and play soccer at an almost professional level (Yule).

As time wore on, it became increasingly clear that Connery would have to choose one hobby over the other. He was unable to score highly in bodybuilding competitions, and he was frequently reminded by other competitors that it was simply untenable for him to continue to play soccer at such a high level while also attempting to add muscle. Even so, he placed third in the Junior category of the 1953 Mr. Universe Competition. On the other hand, Connery's prowess on the soccer field allegedly earned him the opportunity to play for Manchester United, which would have effectively paved the way for an entire career as a professional soccer player. Only a few years after it appeared he was destined to be a laborer in Edinburgh, he had legitimate employment opportunities from which to choose.

Chapter 3: A New Life as An Actor

"If America had been discovered as many times as I have, no one would remember Columbus." – Sean Connery

As Connery's career choice reveals, he ultimately chose not to pursue either hobby professionally and instead decided to pursue acting. In 1951, he had helped out with the stage production at King's Theatre, and the experience instilled in him a passion for acting that had never previously existed. In fact, throughout his childhood Connery had eschewed film and theatre, both due to lack of finances and because his parents showed no interest in them either. Although the experience with the production design at the King's Theatre did not lead him to believe that he had a future in acting, his time spent there resonated with him. At a subsequent bodybuilding competition in 1953, two fellow competitors informed Connery that the stage musical production of *South Pacific* was hiring for chorus boys to essentially serve as extras, and both of these competitors were actors in the show.

The King's Theatre in Edinburgh

Despite having no training in acting, Connery tried out for the role and was accepted. It would be a position that effectively indoctrinated him into the world of theatre and the entertainment industry. Although the medium was different, Connery's job with the production of *South Pacific* was in many ways not entirely dissimilar from his earlier stints as a model and bodyguard. In each case, he was coveted for his body. Given the fact he was playing the role of chorus boy, along with the subsequent appreciation bestowed upon him for his baritone speaking voice, it is perhaps surprising that he was hired almost exclusively on the merits of his physique, but at this point in his career he had not received any vocal training. In fact, his audition was quite poor, but director Joshua Logan, who had spent ample time in Hollywood directing film noirs, was impressed by his physical stature (Bray).

As a result, Connery essentially learned how to utilize his voice while on the job, which required giving himself elocution lessons and venturing to other stage performances in order to borrow from the mannerisms of professional actors (Bray). Connery's theatre education was also strengthened by the connections bestowed upon him through his new job. At a party for *South Pacific*, he met fellow young actor Michael Caine, and the two quickly became good friends. Even more influential was the relationship Connery forged with theatre director Robert Henderson, who introduced Connery to seminal literary texts and served as the drama professor he never had. Under Henderson's tutelage, Connery absorbed works by Turgenev, Tolstoy, Proust, Shakespeare, and Joyce, and through familiarizing himself with these canonical literary works, Connery gained the theatrical acumen that would allow him to avoid being appreciated solely for his looks.

Michael Caine and director Sidney Lumet on the set of *Deathtrap*

One of the salient distinctions between working as a theatrical actor and a film actor is that plays have extended runs while films are mechanically reproduced and therefore do not require the artist to perform over and over again before an audience. This distinction was fortuitous for Connery primarily because it meant that he had continuous employment for as long as *South Pacific* remained successful and continued to tour. In 1955, he was given a small speaking part in the production, and by the end of the year, he was a fixture in the London Theatre.

The following year, he entered a romantic relationship with actress Julie Hamilton, and her connections were influential in helping Connery acquire more acquaintances within the industry. Also in 1956, he appeared in several television shows, though none of which are well-known in the present moment. The shows Connery appeared in during 1956 include *The Square Ring*, *The Condemned*, *Epitaph*, and *Dixon of Dock Green*. These programs should be appreciated for the role they played in building Connery's career rather than for any merits they might have on their own, and they are virtually unpalatable for modern viewers. However, by entering television, Connery inched himself one step further toward entering the film industry and rising to greater fame.

Connery's television career brought him into contact with actress Diane Cilento, who starred alongside him in the television production of *Anna Christie*. He and Cilento became romantically involved. In 1957, Sean also hired agent Richard Hatton, who helped him secure more desirable roles and give him the opportunity to appear in studio-distributed films for the first time. Unfortunately for Connery, his earliest appearances were similar in nature to his initial role in *South Pacific*; as he was hired solely by virtue of his impressive physical attributes. Ironically, Connery's fate early in his career was quite similar to many actresses, who had traditionally been cast largely to satisfy the voyeuristic desires of male viewers, but in his case, Connery's performances were predicated on satisfying the female viewer. His first film appearance had been in 1954, when he held a role as an extra in the 1954 musical *Lilacs in the Spring*, but his first speaking role was in *No Road Back* (1957), a British film directed by Montgomery Tully. The film was never designed for critical success, making it the British equivalent of a B-picture, and Connery's subsequent films fared little better.

Nevertheless, in 1957, Connery signed a contract with 20th Century Fox, officially making him a film actor. Later in 1957, Connery appeared in *Hell Drivers*, an action film in the same vein as *No Road Back*. In his other two films that year, *Action of the Tiger* and *Time Lock*, Connery's roles are similarly minor, and the films were entirely unremarkable. It would not be until 1958, with the production of *Another Time, Another Place*, which starred box office sensation Lana Turner, that Connery would reach greater fame.

Lana Turner

During the late 1950s, Connery was unwilling to commit to a long-term relationship, constantly turning his attention to different women. In 1958, while starring in *Another Time, Another Place*, his most high-profile role to this point, he and Lana Turner had a relationship, even though Turner had her boyfriend, Johnny Stompanato, come across the Atlantic to visit her. Stompanato would later be killed by Turner's daughter during a controversial domestic dispute in Beverly Hills later that year (Bray).

Connery's fun-loving personality, which was almost entirely obscured in later years due to his almost hermetic lifestyle, clashed with the conservative ethos of the British film industry during the time period. In this regard, Michael Feeney Callan notes, "In 1957, when he started in movies, aged 27, British film was culturally limpish and non-representative…the prevailing production spirit was class-driven and, in hindsight, almost offensively anachronistic and the favoured acting style all but Elizabethan. Connery would have none of it…There was nothing saintly about him. He accepted with vigor the prizes of the spotlight: the women, the travel, the money for jam."

There was no question Connery's behavior and acting style broke with tradition. Until he arrived, British cinema had not been so blatant in its celebration of male sexuality, and Connery's fun-loving, playboy spirit was commensurate with his early film portrayals.

Chapter 4: Bond

"I care about Bond and what happens to him. You cannot be connected with a character for this long and not have an interest. All the Bond films had their good points." – Sean Connery

Another Time, Another Place was a watershed film for Connery; even though the plot was a stereotypical 1950s melodrama and antithetical to the action-based persona Connery later cemented. Co-starring alongside Lana Turner meant increased publicity, which in turn would lead to more substantial film appearances. In 1959, he starred in the adventure film *Tarzan's Greatest Adventure*, and though he does not star as Tarzan, Connery was given a major role as the villainous O'Bannion. That same year, he starred in the Disney production *Darby O'Gill and the Little People* (1959), a modestly acclaimed film involving a leprechaun's interactions with an Irish town.

In 1961, Connery received another major role in the British late noir film *The Frightened City*. Although the film was produced in Britain, it was also distributed in the United States and incrementally raised Connery's fame on the other side of the Atlantic. Also adding to Connery's career was a small role in the famous war film *The Longest Day*; while his part was quite small, appearing in such a well-regarded film demonstrated that Connery could appear in a serious film that didn't simply capitalize on his appearance.

Connery in *The Frightened City*

Despite some major developments in the wake of *Another Time, Another Place*, Connery's career was not progressing as rapidly as he desired. In this vein, it is telling that *Another Time, Another Place* was not actually distributed by 20th Century Fox but instead by Paramount, meaning Connery was loaned by his parent studio to Paramount. As a result, in 1962 Connery was attracted by the opportunity of working with another studio, and he was given the chance to audition for *Dr. No*, a film adaptation of Ian Fleming's serial novel involving the James Bond action hero. Initially, Connery was reticent to play Bond, because he was leery about appearing in what would be a series of films, and Diane Cilento, whom he would marry in 1962, had more highbrow tastes and did not care for the Bond series (Pfeifer and Lisa). However, Connery's career had not yet reached the point where he could afford to turn down a potentially lucrative opportunity, so he agreed to audition for the part of James Bond.

Diane Cilento

In addition to Connery's initial reluctance, casting him was a controversial decision for producers Harry Saltzman and Albert R. Broccoli, and allegedly, the producers would never have even considered him had it not been for the efforts of Broccoli's wife (Yule). Another skeptic was the author of the Bond novels himself, Ian Fleming. Fleming had modeled his own character's looks off the actor Hoagy Carmichael, so there was nothing Connery could have done to convince Fleming, but with a large budget of over $1 million, there would have been a vigorous debate regardless of who was cast in the starring role. Still, when considering that

Connery's most significant film to this date had been a generic melodrama nearly four years earlier, it is easy to see why plenty of people doubted the producers' decision to cast Connery in a film featuring him as a suave action hero. Connery himself understood the doubts, telling Playboy magazine in a 1965 interview, "Before I got the part, I might have agreed with them. If you had asked any casting director who would be the sort of man to cast as Bond, an Etonbred Englishman, the last person into the box would have been me, a working-class Scotsman. And I didn't particularly have the face for it; at 16 I looked 30, although I was never really aware of age until I was in my 20s. When I was acting with Lana Turner I realized suddenly I was 28 - -and I'm even more aware of time and age now than I was then. But today my face is accepted as Bond, and that's how it should be."

Hoagy Carmichael

Fleming's own sketch of James Bond

Ian Fleming

From the very beginning, Connery had to overhaul his mannerisms to successfully embody the role of James Bond, because up to this point in his career, he was considered by many to be a boorish action hero or simply a handsome body used as a sideshow attraction. Director Terrence Young took Connery under his tutelage, working with the actor to completely change the way in which he comported himself. Connery had previously behaved in a gruff physical manner, exemplified in his role in the Tarzan film, but portraying Bond required a more delicate touch, even while still retaining the virile sexual appeal that made Bond a charmingly successful womanizer. After first being informed of Connery's hiring, Ian Fleming had noted that he did not see how the rough Connery could portray the debonair Bond, but under Young's guidance, Connery pulled off the complete transformation. Connery discussed some of what it entailed, explaining, "What had to be seized on, in playing a special agent like Bond, were certain immediates such as dress, physical ability, humor, coolness in dangerous situations…"

Published from 1953-1965, the James Bond books were a fundamental component of pop culture in the United States and Great Britain. In an era of Cold War anxiety, Bond's assured masculinity as a British secret agent was a soothing respite. Had Connery's performance been over aggressive, the character would have fed into Cold War paranoia rather than exhibiting the self-confidence that made the novels famous. While the enduring popularity of the Bond films has largely removed them from their original context, it is important to remember that the James Bond novels and films were very much born out of a historical moment filled with mass hysteria. Connery himself seemed to understand the allure of Bond, and he credited the era for Bond's success in the Playboy interview: "Well, timing had a lot to do with it. Bond came on the scene after the War, at a time when people were fed up with rationing and drab times and utility clothes and a predominately gray color in life. Along comes this character who cuts right through all that like a very hot knife through butter, with his clothing and his cars and his wine and his women. Bond, you see, is a kind of present-day survival kit. Men would like to imitate him - or at least his success - and women are excited by him."

Ordinarily, when a film is adapted from a novel, the reaction of the book's author is of little importance. However, the James Bond novels were an international phenomenon, and it was imperative that Connery adequately embody the character Fleming had portrayed in the books. In retrospect, of course, it seems ludicrous that people would have any doubts about Connery's ability to play Bond, but at the time, the books were extremely popular, and the public's response to the movies would be largely determined by how closely Connery adhered to the character established in the novels. By the time the Bond movies were rousing successes and Connery was inextricably associated with the master spy, Connery actually had to remind people that part of Bond's demeanor could be attributed to Connery's own personality. When asked if he had acquired Bond's traits by playing the role, he explained in the Playboy interview, "I like to think I acquired them before Bond. But I am much more experienced as a film actor; that's for sure. And I do play golf now, which I never did before. I started after *Dr. No*, not so much because Bond and Fleming were golfers, but because I couldn't play football as much as I used to, and golf is a game you can play until you're 90."

Although it's hardly the most famous of the series, the first Bond film, *Dr. No* (1962), was a major box office hit and proved that Connery would be an excellent fit for not only the first film but future ones in the series as well. It was one of the first films to open with saturation booking, debuting in Great Britain before opening in the United States, but the film was immensely successful across the world. The plot, which featured Connery in the iconic starring role as a British special agent and also starred Ursula Andress and Joseph Wiseman, involved Bond traveling to Jamaica to investigate the assassination of a fellow British special agent. While on the trail for his colleague's killer, he is alerted to the actions of the eponymous criminal mastermind, Dr. Julius No, who intends to use a radio beam to threaten an American mission in outer space. The genius of the narrative lay in its stylish and light parody of international events that had fueled American anxieties over the preceding decade. America was still in the wake of the hysteria-fueled events of the Red Scare, replete with the House Un-American Activities Committee and the careful censoring of all film and pop culture literature. For the contemporary audience, it was liberating watch an action hero suavely navigate even the most dire of circumstances.

Connery as James Bond in *Dr. No*

The Cold War subtext of the Bond films made them the 1950s equivalent of the war films that had been so popular in the previous decade during World War II. To this end, Michael Denning argues that "the spy novel (and film) is in a sense the war novel of the Cold War" (57). Moreover, Denning identifies how James Bond helped shift the thriller genre from the margins of Hollywood cinema (manifesting mainly through Warner Brothers gangster films) to the forefront: "With James Bond, the spy thriller enters its moment of greatest popularity. Whereas earlier we found espionage themes coming to dominate the thriller generally, we now see the espionage thriller coming to dominate the entire field of popular fiction. Tales of spies are no longer one part of popular culture; they are at its centre. James Bond transcended the novels and films which brought him to life, and joined that small group of fictional characters who are known by many who never read or saw the 'original' texts—figures like Robinson Crusoe and Sherlock Holmes." (56).

In essence, Connery's portrayal of James Bond not only impacted the films in which he appeared but had a decisive influence on the motion picture industry as a whole, and in the process Bond and the genre became fixtures of pop culture. Connery's Bond was a screen phenomenon, but also a sociological one as well.

Dr. No and the subsequent Bond films had a salient political message concerning the abatement of Cold War anxieties, but they were influential on a cultural level as well. The global travel undertaken by Bond made the film a sort of travelogue that displayed the hero's ability to jet-set from one location to the next. Moreover, the Bond films were also significant for rendering sexuality more explicit in cinema and popular culture. While sexuality had become more pronounced over the preceding decade and a half with the population of the film noir genre, the Bond films overtly portrayed sexual relations between men and women without attaching a negative moral connotation to the act. The womanizing Bond not only engages in sometimes kinky sexual activity but does so while retaining his desirability and avoids being characterized as a pervert. Discussing the cultural significance of Bond and the legacy he engendered, Michael Feeney Callan argues, "Sean Connery played a major role in the creation of a modern myth of almost Jungian proportions. He came out of provincial Britain at a time of austerity to create a cornerstone of the Hedonism of the 60s and help change the fortunes of British cinema. He was a dynamic force, seemingly self-made, at the centre of a cultural hurricane."

While Callan exaggerates the extent to which the Bond character was self-made by Connery, he properly identifies the immense effect that Bond had on popular culture. Suddenly, it became acceptable for risqué sexuality to appear throughout British and American culture as a whole, and not only in media and film. Bond was not only a movie character but one to be emulated.

It is true that the Bond films had a transformative effect on American and British cultures, but at the same time, it is easy to see which other films influenced them, and the Bond films should not be heralded as entirely innovative or unique. In fact, in one book-length study on Alfred Hitchcock, Robin Wood chastises the Bond films for being poor imitations of Hitchcock's *North*

By Northwest (1959), and the Bond films also owe a heavy debt to the serial films of the early 20th century that featured adventure hero protagonists involved in jingoistic plots. As other critics have noted, Wood had his own agenda to promote in criticizing the Bond films, namely his own adulation and promotion of Hitchcock, but for those who have viewed Hitchcock's film, it is difficult not to compare Connery's role to that of Cary Grant in *North By Northwest*. While it is perhaps unfair to declare the Bond films a pathetic imitation of Hitchcock, the comparison illuminates the manner in which subsequent films borrow from the successful elements of past movies.

If Wood and other highbrow film scholars were largely disapproving of the Bond series, it has also been argued that the series was revolutionary in its subject matter, largely due to the explicitness through which sexuality is conveyed. In this vein, Callan contends, "Connery's James Bond was much more than a rethreaded adventure/spy formula: it was a new genre, a place of transgressed boundaries and fused polarities, where sadomasochistic sexuality was made palatable by virtue of the subtlest wit, where pyrotechnics muscled in on the Aristotelian principles of drama—and it was universally alluring most of all for the virtuosity of its core character, a sole actor: Connery."

Callan's argument clarifies the central distinction between the Bond films and its predecessors. While Hitchcock's *North By Northwest* featured sexuality, it surfaced more through innuendo and did not involve the overt nature of the Bond movies. The iciness of Hitchcock's women, including Kim Novak (*Vertigo* (1958)), Eva Marie Saint (*North By Northwest*) and Grace Kelly (*Rear Window* (1954) and *To Catch a Thief* (1955)), contrasted sharply with the more sexually explicit portrayals of the Bond girls.

A discussion of sexuality in the Bond films leads to an area that has historically attracted a great deal of attention and drawn the ire of academic circles: the films' treatment of women. A repeated motif of each film is the preponderance of scantily-clad women, epitomized at the very beginning by Ursula Andress' character in *Dr. No*. Moreover, while Bond is smooth and even-keeled in public, he frequently dominates his women, many of whom are objectified in the formal technique of the Bond films, with many shots lingering on the attractive women. There may be no greater example of cinematic voyeurism than the Bond films, as the viewer inhabits the male gaze of Bond himself and women are in a sense portrayed as little more than beautiful décor. Meanwhile, Connery's character was glorified to an almost unparalleled degree in the history of Hollywood cinema, and it is the magnetism of his character that has led to the series' continued popularity.

These themes have led to persuasive arguments that the films are not far removed from soft-core pornography. For example, Michael Denning sees the Bond films as the cinematic continuation of a cultural movement centering on "mass pornography" that surfaced through the Bond novels and publications such as *Playboy*: "what characterizes these representations and the era of mass pornography are, first, a narrative structured around the look, the voyeuristic eye, coding woman as its object, and second, a culture whose every discourse is dominated by, indeed translated into, a code of sexual signifiers" (70). Obviously, films such as *Dr. No* deviate from pornography due to the presence of a more meaningful and significant plotline, but Denning's argument locates the manner in which the Bond films are formulaically geared toward pausing at opportune moments to lust over the sexy bodies of the actresses on screen. James Bond may be a transcendent character, but there is no doubt that the sexual politics of the series hold the potential to alienate female viewers.

In the end, *Dr. No* had a major impact on the film industry and culture as a whole. Before James Bond, films had not combined international politics with brazen sexuality in such a manner, and to a degree, the Bond films were an amalgamation of different currents of pop culture that had surfaced over the previous decade. It would not be inaccurate to frame it as the conflation of *Playboy* and *MAD* magazine, for example. Even the fiercest advocates of the film's production could not have anticipated the box office explosion that erupted from *Dr. No*, making the franchise a major coup for United Artists.

Before *Dr. No*, Connery had struggled to cement his niche as an actor, and the remainder of his career would largely be spent attempting to dissociate himself from his role. In the five years following the release of *Dr. No* in 1962, Connery would appear in four additional Bond films. The first of these was *From Russia with Love*, which was released in 1963 and is recognized by many as the most successful film of the entire Bond canon. The plot features Bond defending himself against the woman to whom he is attracted, combining romantic relations with international intrigue. Evaluating films based on their box office receipts is a dubious venture, and there are scores of superlative films that never received ample attention at the box office, but the success of *From Russia with Love* cemented the importance of the James Bond series as a cultural phenomenon. *Dr. No* was a difficult act to follow, but *From Russia with Love* easily surpassed the previous film in popularity and further demonstrated the emergence of the spy thriller as a viable film genre.

The remaining three Bond films in which Connery appeared over the course of the decade — *Goldfinger* (1964), *Thunderball* (1965), and *You Only Live Twice* (1967) — all performed superbly at the box office and ably carried on the series. Each film was introduced through a sophisticated, high-powered marketing campaign that laid the framework for later film series such as *Jaws* (1975) and *Star Wars* (1977). At the same time, what the series accomplished in terms of repeatable success it lost in critical reception. As discussed earlier, *Dr. No* was no darling of the critics, but the later Bond films were criticized for their formulaic nature. Making matters worse was the fact that the 1960s was a time in which the international art house cinema was in full effect. Through the influence of the French *Cahiers du Cinema*, as well as American critics such as Andrew Sarris, film studies gained legitimacy as an area of academic study. With this increased respectability, the public and critics alike began looking for the mark of an *auteur*, or a directorial signature. James Chapman notes, "The Bond films, with their formula-based plots, standardized narratives and stereotyped characters, were regarded as a sort of film-making by numbers, the antithesis of the cinema of personal expression exemplified by *auteurs* like Hitchcock" (9). Because the Bond films were dominated by their star rather than the director (Terence Young directed just three of the Bond films during the 1960s), the films were thus robbed of critical acclaim that may well have been bestowed on them had they been released prior to the *auteur*-focused bent in film studies that developed over the early 1960s.

An Astor Martin DB5 was the famous Bond car in *Goldfinger*

The James Bond series was obviously instrumental in furthering Connery's career, but he had difficulty establishing an identity distinct from the secret agent. During the Bond years (1962-1967), he also appeared in a handful of other films, most notably the Hitchcock film *Marnie* (1964). That film is now recognized as a critical success, championed above all by Robin Wood, one of the Bond films' greatest critics, but it was difficult for contemporary viewers to embrace after having so thoroughly associated Connery with Bond. The somewhat esoteric subject matter, centering on an epileptic blonde's struggle to overcome childhood trauma, was also a difficult one and out of line with the more tightly constructed narratives for which Hitchcock was famous. However, the main critique of *Marnie* was that Connery was a poor leading man for a Hitchcock film, and it is difficult to watch the film without filtering the character through the prism of James Bond. Viewers saw his character as a poor rendering of James Bond rather than appreciating the film on its own merits.

In truth, the film's lukewarm reception was largely due to Hitchcock's own shortcomings, not Connery, but the star's failure to appear in a successful film by an acclaimed director furthered the stigma that Connery was not an accomplished actor. In the end, Hitchcock himself was also negatively impacted by the popularity of the Bond films, as movies such as *Torn Curtain* (1965) were seen as lackluster variations on the spy thriller Bond narratives (Kapsis). While Bond was identified by some as a poor imitation of Hitchcock, some of the late films by the venerable master of suspense were seen as poor renderings of the Bond movies.

For his own part, Connery was proud of *Marnie*, and ironically, given the way in which people couldn't disassociate Connery from Bond, he talked to Playboy about fan mail he got from Americans that seemed to turn the notion on its head: "I got some nice letters also about Marnie, the Hitchcock film, where I played an American. I think one of the reasons they accept me over there is that most of the younger British actor today, like Finney and O'Toole and me, are more organic, down-to-earth actors than previous generations. In America and Canada and places like that, where they are still breaking through, they appreciate and accept organic acting more readily and enthusiastically. In America there is much more feel for realism than in Europe, where there is still a conception of an actor as being somehow divorced from real life, and in Britain, where acting is still often associated more with being statuesque and striking poses and declaiming with lyrical voices. I'm more interested in things that appeal to me and what I think I have a contact with. But I can still appreciate classical acting--like Olivier's Othello."

In another attempt to diversify his acting portfolio, Connery appeared in the 1965 comedy *A Fine Madness*, which was distributed by Warner Brothers and directed by Irvin Keshner. In the zany plot, Connery stars as a poet overcome with writer's block. The film is hardly remembered now, but it displayed Connery's ability to play a character entirely dissimilar from James Bond. The suspenseful nature of *Marnie* was perhaps too close to the territory of the Bond films to truly reflect the range of characters Connery could portray, so appearing as a poet in a comedy was better suited to the task.

Ultimately, the 1960s were a period of great triumph for Connery on both a personal and a professional level. The Bond series made him an international icon, setting a new standard for suave masculinity and giving Connery a position once held by Cary Grant, who was reaching an advanced age. Connery's personal life also flourished during this period; in 1962, he married longtime girlfriend Diane Cilento, and they would remain married until 1973. The year after their marriage, they had a child, Jason. Although he had difficulty distancing himself from James Bond, the domestic lifestyle successfully portrayed an alternate side of the actor that magazines exposed to the public. In a feature on Connery in *Life* magazine from 1964, the article highlights the differences between Connery's persona on the screen and off it:

"On screen he impersonates the suave secret agent with well-iced perfection;

off-camera, he bears as much semblance to champagne-sipping Bond as a bowlfull of haggis to *jambon en croute*…Despite film successes which will earn him close to a million a year, the off-camera Connery has remained so staunchly unpretentious and un-Bondlike that one suspects some sort of dour Scottish joke. Either that, or Connery—a gifted actor—is trying to transmit the simply subliminal message that he cannot bear to be bottled in Bond, even at a quarter-million dollars a shot." (55).

Chapter 5: Moving Beyond Bond

As Connery's off-screen persona became more recognized, it became more possible for moviegoers to envision him in roles other than James Bond. After the completion of *You Only Live Twice* in 1967, he took a four-year hiatus from the series and built a separate screen identity. Also contributing to the decision to break his commitment to the series was a lack of creative control. After it was clear that the series was successful, Connery yearned for a stake in United Artists, hoping to occupy a three-way monopoly over the studio alongside Broccoli and Saltzman, the two producers of the Bond films. Instead, he was relegated to the status of well-paid star, and not even included in the profit-sharing until the release of *Goldfinger* in 1964. The resultant friction with Broccoli and Saltzman, as well as the need to diversify, fueled his decision to break away from Bond.

At the start of the 1970s, Connery was entering his 40s, a time in which many actors begin to find difficulty securing starring roles. However, Sean was blessed that as he grew older, he maintained his muscular physique, and plenty of people believed that he grew even more attractive with each passing year. The sly, boyish grin associated with James Bond gave way to a more mature, stately appearance.

But curiously, as he grew older, Connery became even less selective with regard to the roles he accepted, a dynamic he shared with good friend Michael Caine. The initial films he appeared in after *You Only Live Twice* returned to the rugged action hero turf he had inhabited prior to James Bond. In 1968, he starred in *Shalako*, a bizarre British Western directed by aging director Edward Dmytryk and co-starring Brigitte Bardot. Two years later, he starred as a coal miner in *The Molly Maguires*, a historical epic set in 19th century Ireland. The latter was a minor critical success but performed miserably at the box office, indicating Connery could no longer count on the legacy from his James Bond films to guarantee a strong public reception. He either had to reinvent his image or return to the role of James Bond.

As Connery's popularity began to wane, he chose to accept nearly every offer that came his way. This included a return to James Bond, in the well-received *Diamonds Are Forever* (1971). However, the same year that the Bond film was released, he also starred in two other movies, *The Red Tent* and *The Anderson Tapes*. For such a high-profile actor to appear in three films in the same year was highly unusual, but it speaks to how Connery managed his stardom differently from other major stars. While most stars are careful not to lend their face to a film that is risky critically or commercially, by appearing in so many films Connery gave the impression that he did not take his own stardom too seriously. This was almost certainly a reflection of his impoverished upbringing, and his work ethic. Connery refused to let money sit on the table, and his distinguished acting style lent respectability to otherwise mediocre films such as *Zardoz* (1974) and *Ransom* (1975). When word got around that Connery was miserly when it came to spending money, he turned back to his past, telling Playboy:

> "I'm not stingy, but I'm careful with it. I don't throw my money around, because money gives you power and freedom to operate as you want. I have respect for its value, because I know how hard it is to earn and to keep. I come from a background where there was little money and we had to be content with what there was. One doesn't forget a past like that... I bought a secondhand Jaguar, and I bought the house I now live in, with about an acre of land; but I don't invest in land, and I don't have a lot of servants--just a secretary and a nanny for the children. Old habits die hard. Even today, when I have a big meal in a restaurant, I'm still conscious that the money I'm spending is equal to my dad's wages for a week. I just can't get over that, even though I sign the bill and don't actually pay in cash. But I still prefer the feel of real money to a checkbook. And I'm still the sort of fellow who hates to see a light left on in a room when no one is there."

While many of Connery's films fell well short of masterpiece status, he did not appear in terrible films either. He starred in many worthwhile pictures and collaborated with respected actors and directors. In 1975, he appeared in the John Huston film *The Man Who Would Be King*, an adaptation of the famous Rudyard Kipling tale. The film, which was nominated for four Academy Awards, gave him the chance to act alongside close friend Michael Caine, and the highbrow script enhanced Connery's standing as an actor capable of appearing in serious films. The following year, Connery starred in an adaptation of *Robin and Marian* (1976), which chronicled the romance between Robin Hood and Lady Marian. Playing Lady Marian was Audrey Hepburn, and the duo received praise for their chemistry.

By the mid-1970s, Connery's marriage to Diane Cilento had suffered, and they obtained a divorce in 1973. After the breakup, Cilento would complain, "The whole damn Bond thing took over our lives." But in ensuing years, Cilento would also claim Connery was physically and verbally abusive to her, and Connery responded to the accusations by deeming her "insane". The sniping between the two was going on as late as 2008, when Cilento accused Connery of refusing to support their son and Connery replying, "Diane can't move on from the break-up of our marriage and I have already had to contend with her accusations about me being violent towards her...Now the lies seem to be getting even more vicious, and, what is worse, she is dragging our son into it." The relationship was irreparably ruined, and continued to be so until Cilento died in 2011.

In 1975, Connery married the Franco-Moroccan painter Micheline Roquebrune, to whom he remains married to this day. He later joked, "I met my wife through playing golf. She is French and couldn't speak English and I couldn't speak French, so there was little chance of us getting involved in any boring conversations - that's why we got married really quickly." It was the kind of quote that would make most people cringe if it wasn't coming out of the mouth of Sean Connery, who had earned a label for making controversial statements about women as far back as the 1960s.

Having married Roquebrune, Connery's domestic life quieted dramatically, and he settled into a more mature, middle-age lifestyle. But one thing Connery's second marriage did not change was his prolific output. He continued to maintain a demanding work schedule, averaging at least one film per year and sometimes multiple films a year. He attributed it to his restlessness, and his desire to travel, relaying one anecdote in the Playboy interview:

> "With their far-flung locations, the Bond films help to satiate it. But to give you an idea how great the hunger is, I was in bed with the flu on a Friday morning in London about three years ago and I got a telephone call and I was chatting away for about 20 minutes before I realized it was Toronto on the line. My first thought was, "My God, I hope he hasn't reversed the charges!" Then he said, "We're doing Macbeth on Monday. Would you like to play it? I said, "What, this Monday?" and he said, "Yes, get a plane and come over. It's a special cultural thing on TV and there's not a lot of money in it"--which seems always the actors' bait. I was to get $500 or so for it. So I said, "Give me an apartment and enough money to live on while I'm there so I don't have to steal food," and he said all right and would I get the plane that afternoon. And there I was, in bed at 11:30 in the morning with flu and I jumped up and said to myself, "Christ--what do I do first?" The first thing was to read the play. So I sat down and read it and suddenly realized what I'd bitten off. It was monumental. I reread it over and over all the way to Canada and somehow I was ready to go on Monday morning."

Despite his work ethic, the films Connery starred in from 1975-1985 were critical failures, including a final turn as James Bond in *Never Say Never Again* (1983). This final Bond appearance is commonly recognized as the weakest of his Bond films, and at the age of 55 he had clearly become too old for the role. His performance also suffered from the fact that viewers could remember Connery's earlier Bond films from two decades prior, when he was more convincing in the role and performing in better Bond movies.

It was not until the late 1980s that Connery began once again appearing in more critically-acclaimed films. In 1987, he was honored with an Academy Award for his supporting role in *The Untouchables*, in which he plays a police officer during Prohibition. The film was the ideal fit for Connery given his age; no longer tasked with portraying youthful playboys, he exudes an experienced air of authority in his role. The movie also afforded him the opportunity to act alongside Robert de Niro and Kevin Costner, and under the direction of Brian de Palma. Although it was the first and only film for which he won an Oscar, Connery's acting is not drastically superior in *The Untouchables* than to his previous roles. Instead, the Academy Award win owed a great deal to the collaborative talents of those with whom he worked with on the film.

After *The Untouchables*, Connery continued to appear in films produced for a mass audience, although this did not preclude critical praise. In 1989, he played the role of Professor Henry Jones Senior in *Indiana Jones and the Last Crusade*, for which he was nominated for a BAFTA Award for Best Actor in a Supporting Role. The next year, he was again nominated for a BAFTA Award, this time for Best Actor in a Leading Role for his performance in *The Hunt for Red October*. In these films, Connery truly begins showing his age, unabashedly wearing a very full gray beard, but the look also gave him a wise, professorial appearance. These films in the late 1980s set the standard for the image Connery would have over the remainder of his career, as he appears very much as an elder statesman of the Hollywood elite. Even today, Connery is instantly recognizable for looking much the same way.

During the 1990s, Connery began taking on production roles in several of the films in which he appeared. In the 1993 film *Rising Sun*, he not only acted but also served as Executive Producer. The film, which features Connery in the familiar role of a retired cop sent to investigate a murder, was a critical failure but a major box office hit. Later in the decade, Connery took production roles in other films of his, including *Just Cause* (1995), *The Rock* (1996), and *Entrapment* (1999), but none of these films were critical successes and are all largely forgotten less than two decades later.

Despite the lukewarm critical response to these films, as well as the fact that he was in his sixties, Connery's productivity still refused to wane. He acted in a total of 14 films during the decade, many of which he held starring roles and production responsibilities.

Chapter 6: Retirement

Connery at the 2008 Edinburgh International Film Festival.

"I'm what I always have been: a Scot, a bit introspective; I don't tell lies and I prefer straight dealing. I don't lose my temper often, except at incompetence--my own or others'. Or when I play golf badly. But I never lose my temper at work; if I have a row there I have a head like ice. I have learned to rely on myself--and to keep my own counsel--since I started earning at 13. Like all Celts, I have my moods, and I'm not particularly generous with them. I rather like to keep them to myself; but if people want to infringe on a mood they are welcome to any part of it. I suppose you could say I am more introvert than extrovert. The extrovert side is in my work." – Sean Connery

It would not be until the last decade that Connery eased into retirement. His last great critical success was in *Finding Forrester* (2000), which featured him in the role of an elderly hermetic writer. Connery shows his age in the role — the film was produced at the time of his 70th birthday — but his appearance, which recalls a well-groomed Ernest Hemingway, remains as stately as ever. The plot involves a mentorship and friendship between Connery and an African-American teenager, with Connery's character guiding the teenager and helps the teen develop as a writer in his own right. That said, *Finding Forrester* might be best known for spawning a Connery-related meme on the Internet, based on his much-parodied quote, "You're the man now, dog." The quote spawned the notorious Internet site ytmnd.com. Naturally, there are a countless number of Connery memes on the site.

After *Finding Forrester*, Connery entered into semi-retirement and grew increasingly more reclusive, as though his character from his last film had rubbed off on him. In many ways, the mysterious nature of Connery's ways and personality became fodder for comedy, perhaps most memorably in *Saturday Night Live* skits that portray Connery playing *Jeopardy* and giving host Alex Trebek a hard time.

Connery's next project was the 2003 film *The League of Extraordinary Gentlemen*, a critical disaster featuring Connery in a starring role as an aging adventure hero. He would act in just one additional film and considered himself retired, but he lent his voice to the film *Sir Billi*, an animated feature in which Connery voiced the part of the eponymous protagonist, a veterinarian.

Over the course of the 21st century, the dominant theme concerning Connery's career has been whether or not he was actually retired. As Connery moved into old age and became more reclusive, he disappeared from the public spotlight and it was assumed that he was retired. Despite being offered countless film opportunities, he turned nearly all of them down, instead electing to retreat to his homes in Greece, the Bahamas, and New York City. Always energetic, Connery continued his active lifestyle, replacing his professional duties with golf, a sport he had played diligently for decades.

Connery's elderly years also involved significant developments in his non-professional life. He became increasingly politically-motivated, supporting Scotland and contributing heavily to the Scottish National Party. He has been vocal in expressing his belief that Scotland should be recognized as an independent nation, and for years remained steadfast in a commitment to never return to Scotland until it gained independence. However, this was dropped in 2008, when he returned to his roots and made an appearance at the Edinburgh Film Festival. In 1997 and 1998, he was nominated for knighthood but denied on the basis of his political affiliation. Finally, in July of 2000 he was awarded knighthood, a designation befitting his revered status in the film industry and reflecting the influence of the James Bond series, but true to form, Connery rather dismissively described the effect being knighted has had on his life: "The knighthood I received was a fantastic honour but it's not something I've ever used and I don't think I ever will."

One consequence of Connery's increasingly secretive nature is that in recent years there has been continued speculation as to not only his retirement but also his death. For the most part, his health has been excellent; in 1989, he suffered from polyps in his throat, although he recovered quickly from the potentially fatal condition (Pfeifer and Lisa). The first rumor that he had passed away was in 1993, when it was falsely declared that he had died as a result of throat cancer from decades of smoking. For the most part, he remained in excellent health for the rest of the decade, and it was not until the 2006 that his health truly began to worsen. That year, he underwent surgery to remove a kidney tumor, and in 2009 he was diagnosed with a heart condition. The next rumor of his death occurred in 2012, but the reports were denied and he continues to spend the majority of his time in the Bahamas.

There is no denying that Sean Connery is above all defined by his performances as James Bond during the 1960s. The James Bond films ushered in a new standard for cool and spawned a genre of sleek spy thrillers. Even though more than five decades have passed since *Dr. No*, the James Bond franchise continues, and for today's actors, being appointed the next James Bond represents the ultimate in chic masculinity, a mantle now held by Daniel Craig in the current Bond films. Connery's legacy is still felt through the Bond films, with successive actors building off his portrayal of the secret agent, and his performances as James Bond inaugurated a more relaxed yet explicit standard for sexuality.

In addition to his Bond legacy, Connery's career is significant for the extent to which he was able to transcend his earlier roles and diversify his career. For many actors, the James Bond films would have robbed them of the opportunity to lead their careers in other directions, and it's perhaps most notable that Connery's Academy Award was won not for his performance in a Bond film but for his supporting role in *The Untouchables*.

One of Connery's great accomplishments was his ability to age gracefully before the camera, leading Bob McCabe to proclaim:

> "Age has not withered him: neither his lack of hair, nor his continued insistence on playing everything from a Russian submarine commander to a fourteenth-century monk, from a Prohibition-era Irish-American street cop to the world's most famous Eton-educated spy, all complete with a thick Edinburgh accent...Connery has instead crafted a career based on a subtle redefining of image that has allowed him to move from sex symbol to character actor, from reborn hero to respected father figure, from adventurer in his youth, to adventurer in his middle age and beyond." (10).

As McCabe notes, Connery's flexibility is one of his defining attributes. While some could denigrate his decision to accept roles that other actors would deem beneath them, it is also worth noting that Connery's prolific output is matched by few actors in Hollywood cinematic history.

To those unfamiliar with him, the expansive scope of Connery's career is perhaps surprising. And while it's largely attributable to his upbringing in a poor tenement in Edinburgh, the fact that he came so far and accomplished so much given that disadvantageous start makes his life and career all the more remarkable. Connery remained active until long after most people choose to retire, and he lent an air of respectability to films that were otherwise entirely forgettable. That Connery was knighted in 2000 not only speaks to his significance in Great Britain's cultural heritage but also reflects his standing in the entertainment realm, and he will forever be remembered for his royal standing within international film history.

Bibliography

Alexander, Shane. "New James Movie: In From Russia with Love, an Unlikely Actor Portrays the Suave Spy." *Life* 3 April 1964: 51-60.

Bray, Christopher. *Sean Connery: A Biography*. New York: Open Road Media, 2011.

Callan, Michael Feeney. *Sean Connery*. New York: Random House, 2012.

Chapman, James. *License to Thrill: A Cultural History of the James Bond Films*. New York: Columbia University Press, 2000.

Denning, Michael. "Licensed to Look: James Bond and the Heroism of Consumption." *The James Bond Phenomenon: A Critical Reader*. Ed. Christopher Lindner. Manchester: Manchester University Press, 2003. 56-75.

Kapsis, Robert E. *Hitchcock: The Making of a Reputation*. Chicago: University of Chicago Press, 1992.

McCabe, Bob. *Sean Connery: A Biography*. New York: Thunder's Mouth Press, 2000.

Parker, John. *Arise Sean Connery: The Biography of Britain's Greatest Living Actor*. London: John Blake, 2009.

Pfeifer, Lee, and Philip Lisa. *The Films of Sean Connery*. New York: Kensington Publishing, 2001.

Wood, Robin. *Hitchcock's Films Revisited*. New York: Columbia University Press, 2002.

Yule, Andrew. *Sean Connery: From 007 to Hollywood Icon*. New York: Dutton Adult, 1992.

Made in the USA
Las Vegas, NV
25 March 2021